Jim Thorpe

YOUNG ATHLETE

Jim Thorpe
YOUNG ATHLETE

by Laurence Santrey
illustrated by George Ulrich

Troll Associates

Library of Congress Cataloging in Publication Data

Santrey, Laurence.
 Jim Thorpe, young athlete.

 Summary: Traces the early life of the Oklahoma
Indian farm boy who achieved a unique sports career as
winner of Olympic gold medals in the pentathlon and
decathlon and as a professional baseball and football
player.
 1. Thorpe, Jim, 1888-1953—Juvenile literature.
2. Athletes—United States—Biography—Juvenile literature. [1. Thorpe, Jim, 1888-1953. 2. Athletes.
3. Indians of North America—Oklahoma—Biography]
I. Ulrich, George, ill. II. Title.
GV697.T5S26 1983   796'.092'4 [B] [92]   82-15982
ISBN 0-89375-845-0
ISBN 0-89375-846-9 (pbk.)

Jim Thorpe

YOUNG ATHLETE

Life was hard for Charlotte and Hiram Thorpe. The land in central Oklahoma, where they lived, was dry and difficult to farm. The Thorpes managed to grow some corn and vegetables, and Mr. Thorpe hunted for meat to put on their table. He also earned a little money taming wild horses for other ranchers in the area. The Thorpe family never went hungry, but they never had very much.

Life was hard for *all* the Indians in the Oklahoma Territory in the late 1800s. They could no longer roam freely over the plains, as Indians had for thousands of years. In the old days, when deer and buffalo became scarce in one place, the Indians traveled to an area where the hunting was better. When their fields did not yield large crops of maize, the Indians moved on to richer land.

But by the 1880s, open land was disappearing. Settlers were moving into Oklahoma. They staked claims to acre after acre of land. They put up fences where Indians used to ride and hunt as free as the wind. They built towns, laid down railroad lines, and brought in their laws and rules. To make room for these newcomers, the Indians were forced onto reservations, sections of government-owned land set aside for Indian tribes.

Charlotte and Hiram Thorpe, who belonged to the Sac and Fox tribe, had a ranch near Shawnee, Oklahoma. There, Hiram had built a two-room cabin. And there, on May 28, 1888, Charlotte gave birth to twin boys. One was named Charles. The other was named James Francis.

The day the boys were born was special in more ways than one to the Thorpes. Exactly 100 years before, Black Hawk—the twins' great-great-grandfather—had been made chief of the Sac and Fox tribe. Black Hawk won fame as a brave and proud warrior. He was also a wise leader.

"I believe the twins will do great things," said Charlotte. "I am sure that my great-grandfather's spirit lives in them."

Hiram Thorpe agreed. "Yes, I think they will be strong, wise, and honorable men one day. And it is our job to see that they grow up that way. As soon as they are old enough to understand, we will tell them about the great Black Hawk and of the noble history of our people."

From the day they were born, Charlie and Jim were always together. Their older brother, George, was away at the reservation school, so the twins did not see him often. Charlie and Jim became very close. They played on the cabin floor, sharing their few toys and talking to each other in the Sac and Fox language. This was the language their parents spoke at home.

The boys were more than just brothers, they were best friends. Once, when the twins were three years old, one of them broke a clay jug filled with milk. Mrs. Thorpe heard the crash and hurried into the cabin.

"I told you boys not to go near the table. Now, who broke the jug?"

The twins looked at her in silence.

"If you don't tell me who did it," Mrs. Thorpe warned, "I will have to punish both of you."

The boys kept silent. Each one was ready to be punished rather than tell on his brother. Finally, Mrs. Thorpe had to spank them. Afterward, she told Jim and Charlie, "I am glad that you love each other so much and are so loyal to each other. But I know you did not like being spanked. So you must learn a lesson from this: Don't let your brother do something wrong, because both of you will be punished for it."

Charlie and Jim learned their lesson. After that, they did not get into trouble very often. Besides, they were too busy playing in the fields or in the

barn. The only time they came into the cabin was
when Mrs. Thorpe called them in for meals or for
bed. The two sturdy little boys were always on
the go.

When the boys were three years old, Mr. Thorpe taught them to ride a pony Indian-style, with no saddle. Until Mr. Thorpe was sure the boys were safe on horseback, he didn't let them ride unless he was with them. But the day soon came when he told them they could ride whenever they wanted. "You don't need me around," he said. "Just make sure you look after each other." And they did.

Mr. Thorpe also made bows and arrows for his sons. Then he took them out into a field and taught them to shoot. "You must never point an arrow at anything unless you are going to shoot," he told them. "And you must never point an arrow at a person."

"But, Pa," four-year-old Jim said. "Didn't Black Hawk and the other braves of our tribe shoot arrows in battle?"

"Yes, my son, but that was very long ago," Mr. Thorpe answered. "Now the Indians are peaceful. There are other reasons for learning to use a bow and arrow. It will teach you to be patient. It will give you strength of arm, a steady hand, and a sharp eye."

Mr. Thorpe set up a bale of hay in the field. Then he showed the boys how to fit the arrow against the bowstring, how to draw it back smoothly, and how to aim at the target. Jim and Charlie practiced shooting for hours every day. At first, their arrows flew wide of the target or fell to the ground.

The boys didn't give up. Each one wanted Mr. Thorpe to praise him. And each one wanted to do better than his twin. If Charlie shot an arrow close to the bale of hay, Jim didn't stop until he shot one even closer. In a short time, both twins became skillful archers.

Doing well in sports was very important to the Thorpe boys. They wanted to be just like their father. Big Hiram, as he was called by his friends, weighed 230 pounds, stood 6 feet 2 inches tall, and had muscles as hard as stones. He was the finest athlete for miles around, and Charlie and Jim saw proof of this all the time.

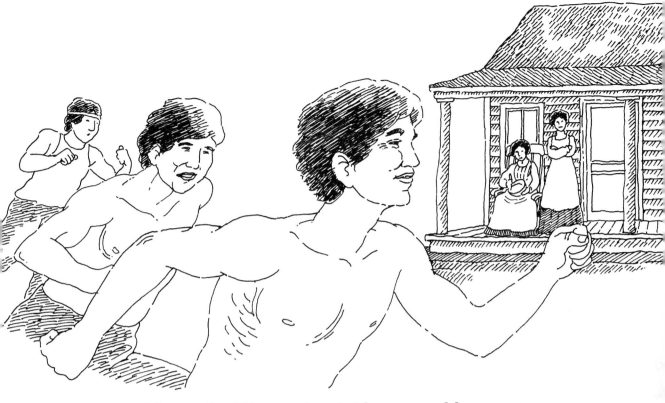

Often, the Thorpes' neighbors would come to visit after the day's work was done. While the women gathered in the cabin or sat in the front yard, the men got together near the barn. There, with a lot of teasing and joking, they challenged each other to different tests of strength and speed.

This was an old Indian tradition. Back in the days of their grandfathers, there were contests like these all the time. The young braves would win fame and admiration for being the best athletes in their tribe.

Like the Indians of long ago, Hiram and his friends competed at running, wrestling, high-jumping, long-jumping, and throwing. Sometimes, when the weather was really hot, they'd go down to the nearby North Canadian River and have swimming races. In all of these contests, Big Hiram was usually the winner.

Jim and Charlie were very proud of their father. Years later, Jim said of him, "He could lick any man in our part of the country in wrestling. I have never known a man with such energy. He could walk, ride, and run for days without ever showing the least sign of fatigue."

That was the way the Thorpe boys saw their father, and that was the model they tried to follow. Jim and Charlie had their own contests in front of the barn. When their brother, George, was home from the reservation school, he also competed. Since George was seven years older than the twins, he always won.

George was much too big for Jim or Charlie to beat at wrestling, but running was something else. In a foot race, he didn't beat them by very much. Even though Jim was short and thin, he was fast! What's more, he hated to lose, and he never gave up trying to be the best. Once, after a really close race, he said, "I'm going to be so fast some day that nobody will outrun me. You'll see!"

Mr. Thorpe was glad that his boys did so well in sports. He spent as much time as he could teaching them how to catch a ball, how to swim, and how to get off to a fast start in a race. Mrs. Thorpe also spent a lot of time with the twins. They loved to hear her stories about the Sac and Fox tribe, and about Chief Black Hawk. They especially liked to hear the Indian legends Charlotte's mother had told her when she was a child.

The Thorpes spent a lot of time with the boys not only because they loved their children, but because they knew that Jim and Charlie would be leaving home soon. When the twins were six years old, they went to live at a boarding school twenty-three miles away, in the middle of the reservation. They stayed there most of the year, coming home only for vacations.

When the Thorpe brothers went off to school, they spoke almost no English. Like most Indian children of that time, they knew only the language of their tribe. At the school, however, Indian languages were not allowed. All classes were taught in English. This way, the teachers hoped, the children would learn to be part of the outside world.

Some of the Indian boys and girls, who were educated at reservation schools, did well. But many did not. They missed the warmth and love of home. And when they were ordered not to speak the language of their parents or follow Indian customs, they felt sad and confused.

Jim did not like living at the school. He missed his mother and father. He missed the freedom of riding a pony over the open fields, of swimming and fishing and shooting arrows at targets. But at least he was with Charlie, so it wasn't all that bad. The twins bunked next to each other in the big room where all the boys slept. They played together and studied together. Jim couldn't feel too homesick as long as Charlie was around.

In their first year at school, the boys learned to speak English and to read and write a little. Jim was never the best student in the class, but outside, on the playground, things were different. There, even though he was one of the smallest boys, he was a star. Jim was the fastest runner, the longest jumper, and the best thrower and hitter in the baseball games—a fine, all-around athlete.

Although Jim was usually a little better at every game they played, Charlie was a good athlete, too. Together, they were unbeatable. Whenever sides were picked for a game, the Thorpe boys were always chosen first. And any team that got both of them was a sure winner.

For Jim and Charlie, the happiest time of the year was when they went home for summer vacation. The golden days of summer were filled with riding, swimming, and playing on the ranch. There were parents to hug and kiss and old friends to see. It was good to be a part of the Indian community again.

Their second year at school was easier than the first. The boys knew how to speak English, so the classwork wasn't as difficult as before. And they had lots of friends—thanks to Charlie. Charlie always knew the right thing to say to other girls and boys. He had a big, sunny grin, and he never got into fights. Jim was quieter and not as good at making friends.

Even though their second year at school went smoothly, the twins couldn't wait to get home for summer vacation. They were still at school on their eighth birthday, in May of 1896, so they wouldn't get their present until they got home. The present—and it was the greatest thing they could wish for—was to go hunting with Mr. Thorpe. He had promised to teach them how to track animals and use a rifle. Every night, when they got into bed, Jim and Charlie whispered excitedly about the great hunting trip.

But the marvelous birthday present was not to be. Soon after the boys got home, Charlie became ill. He developed a high fever and grew very, very weak. He was sick with pneumonia, a serious infection of the lungs. In those days, before the discovery of drugs like penicillin, there was no cure for pneumonia. Sometimes people got better. More often they died.

For weeks, Charlie lay in bed, getting weaker each day. Jim sat beside the bed hour after hour. He tried to cheer up his brother. He fed Charlie soup or cornmeal in warm milk. He put cool, wet cloths on Charlie's forehead. But nothing helped. Later that summer, Charlie Thorpe died.

Jim was filled with grief. Charlie had been his dearest friend. In all the world, nobody was closer. Mr. and Mrs. Thorpe and Jim's brother George tried to get Jim to talk about his sorrow. But they could not get him to open up or to cry. He sat by himself for hours or went for long, lonely walks. His face was always sad.

Jim missed Charlie even more when he went back to school in the fall. Nothing interested him —not the classwork, not the other boys, not even the games. More and more, Jim was becoming a loner. He went for days without talking to anyone.

One morning, when he could bear it no longer, Jim walked out of the school and started for home. He ran and walked twenty-three miles without stopping. At last, the weary boy reached the Thorpe cabin.

"What's wrong, Jim?" Mrs. Thorpe asked, putting her arms around her son. "Did something happen at school?"

"I hate it there," Jim said. "I miss Charlie, and I want to be home with you. I can help do the chores and anything else you want me to do. Please don't send me back!"

Mrs. Thorpe sighed. "You will miss Charlie wherever you are, Jim. But you have to go back to school. You need an education."

"Why must I go to school?" Jim asked. "You didn't go to school. Pa didn't go. Chief Black Hawk didn't, either."

"Black Hawk was of another time," Mrs. Thorpe answered. "His world is gone. Pa and I didn't go to school when we were your age because there was no school. Now the United States government has built schools for Indians, and the law says we *must* send our children to them. That is why you have to go back right now."

After a quick supper and a kiss from his mother, Jim and his father left the cabin. In the moonlight, side by side, they began the long trip back to the school. While they walked, Mr. Thorpe recalled his own childhood. He spoke of the days when huge herds of buffalo covered the plains for many miles and of the dances the Indians performed on sacred days. Big Hiram also spoke of great contests among the braves, held to decide who was the strongest and the fastest. He talked about his family and the wise men of the tribe. He remembered being taught to be a good member of the tribe, to obey the laws, and to live with honor.

Father and son reached the school just as the sun was rising. At the front door, Mr. Thorpe hugged Jim for a moment. Then he turned and silently began the journey back to the ranch. Jim did not leave school the rest of the year.

But the next year the same thing happened. This time, Mr. Thorpe did not take Jim back to the local reservation school. Instead, he told Jim, "A young brave does not run from what he must do. And you must go to school! So I am going to send you very far away. You will not be able to walk home from there."

A week later, Jim arrived at his new school, the Haskell Institute, in Lawrence, Kansas. At first, he was not happy there, either. Then he met Chauncey Archiquette. Chauncey, one of the older students, was the star of Haskell's football team.

Jim watched the team practice every day. He liked to see Chauncey pass and kick the ball and run past all the players trying to tackle him. After a while, Chauncey noticed the small, thin boy who attended practice every day.

"Do you like football?" Chauncey asked Jim one afternoon.

"I think it's the best game I've ever seen," Jim replied. "I've never played it, but I'd sure like to try. I'm a fast runner, and I'm very strong, too."

The broad-shouldered Archiquette looked at the younger boy. "I don't think you're big enough to play on the school team yet," Chauncey said. "But I'll help you get ready. Every day, after team practice, you and I will work out together. I'll show you some of the things I've learned."

Jim was thrilled to be Archiquette's friend and pupil. And he proved to be a very fast learner. Archiquette even said that Jim would be good enough to make the team as soon as he grew a little bigger. Jim liked that idea. But even more than that, he enjoyed having a friend like Chauncey. For the first time since Charlie's death, Jim didn't feel lonely all the time.

Jim began to enjoy sports again. In fact, as he said years later, sports were the best part of life at Haskell. He certainly wasn't as happy in the

classroom, where many of the teachers treated the
Indian children as if they were not as good as the
other children. This hurt the feelings of the Indian
boys and girls at Haskell. At home, they were told
that it was a fine thing to be an Indian. At
Haskell, they were not encouraged to be proud of
their Indian background.

Jim disliked this, but since he had to be at Haskell, he made the best of it. He never talked back to his teachers, and he stayed out of trouble.

Then, when he was twelve, a note arrived from his mother. It said that Mr. Thorpe had been hurt in a hunting accident and that Jim should come home right away.

The school principal was going to arrange for Jim to take a train home, but the boy could not wait. He packed the few clothes he owned, threw the small bundle over his shoulder, and set out for Shawnee. It was about 250 miles away, and it took Jim two weeks to get there by foot. He lived off the land the whole time.

By the time he got home, Jim's father was well. But there was an even more serious problem— Mrs. Thorpe had become very sick. A few weeks after Jim got home, she died. Grief-stricken, Jim went outside and began to walk around the ranch, remembering all the happy times he had spent with his mother. Then he returned to the cabin and asked his father if he could stay home instead of going back to school. This time, Mr. Thorpe said yes.

For the next three years, Jim helped his father and George on the ranch. He fixed fences, tamed wild horses, plowed and planted and harvested. In that time, Jim grew taller and stronger. He liked being home with his father and George, but every now and then, he thought about the football games at Haskell.

In the summer of 1904, when Jim was sixteen, a man came to visit the Thorpe ranch. He was an official from the United States Industrial School in Carlisle, Pennsylvania. At the school, usually called Carlisle Institute, Indian teenagers were taught useful trades. The man asked Jim if he would like to learn a trade.

"Yes," Jim said. "I'd like to be an electrician."

"I'm sorry, but that is something we do not teach," the official told the boy. "However, we can teach you to be a painter, a carpenter, a tailor, a shoemaker, or many other things."

Jim didn't say anything for a few minutes. He wasn't sure if he wanted to go away again. The man finally broke the long silence. "I hear you're a pretty good athlete," he said. "We have good coaching and fine sports teams at Carlisle. Maybe you can play baseball or football for us."

Now Jim was interested. The idea of competing on a real team sounded wonderful to him. "Okay," he said. "I'll give it a try."

And so, in the fall of 1904, Jim Thorpe entered Carlisle Institute, where he decided to learn the tailoring trade. He also tried out for the football team, but he didn't make it. Jim was disappointed. Still, he understood why he was turned down—he wasn't big enough for the varsity squad. Maybe next year...

Jim grew a few inches in the following year, and he tried very hard to stay in top shape. He worked on local farms during the summer and ran for miles every day, all year long. At last, he was noticed by Glen "Pop" Warner, who coached Carlisle's track and football teams. In the spring of 1906, Warner saw Jim playing in a pick-up football game. Coach Warner liked the way Jim ran and asked him, "Why don't you try out for my track team?"

"I would really like to play on your football team, sir," Jim answered.

"Maybe you can do both, young man," Coach Warner said. "Let's start with track and see what happens."

That year, Jim mastered the high jump, the long jump, and the 100-yard dash. Warner was very pleased with the quiet, determined young man. The coach felt there was something special about the Sac and Fox athlete.

In the fall of 1907, Jim, who was now 6 feet 1 inch tall and weighed 180 pounds, made the varsity football team. He was a star from the opening game. Nobody could stop the powerful, swift runner as he flew down the field, the football clutched against his body. In the spring, he was outstanding both as a runner on the track team and as a slugging outfielder for the Carlisle baseball team. The glorious saga of Jim Thorpe, super-athlete, had begun.

Before his playing days at Carlisle were over, Jim was twice chosen a football All-American. In one game during the 1911 season, Jim was at his best against a tough University of Pittsburgh team. He was a mighty runner all game long. Time and again, his kicking kept Pittsburgh away from Carlisle's goal line. Twice, Jim kicked the ball, ran the length of the field like a deer, and tackled the Pitt player who had caught the ball. And each time, when the tackled player fumbled the ball, Jim scooped it up!

A third time, Jim kicked the ball far downfield, fought off five Pitt players who were scrambling for it, and grabbed the ball. He brushed off tackler after tackler and carried the football 20 yards for a touchdown.

Jim was almost a one-man team that day. Carlisle won the game by a score of 17–0. And by the end of the season, All-American Jim Thorpe led Pop Warner's team to a record of eleven wins with only one loss.

Sports fans were even more thrilled by the superb athlete in 1912. In that year, Jim represented the United States at the Olympic Games. He competed in the pentathlon—made up of five running, jumping, and throwing events. Incredibly, Jim won gold medals in the pentathlon *and* the decathlon—fifteen events in all! As Jim received his second gold medal, King Gustav the Fifth of Sweden remarked to him, "Sir, you are the greatest athlete in the world!"

But the Olympics were for amateur athletes only. A short time later, the Olympic officials learned that, before the Games, Jim had played baseball for a small salary. This made Jim a professional athlete, and so, he could not keep his Olympic medals.

But Jim's sports career was far from over. He played major-league baseball for the New York Giants, Cincinnati Reds, and Boston Braves. He played professional football for the Canton Bulldogs, New York Giants, and Chicago Cardinals. He was also chosen to be the first president of the National Football League.

No one in American history has ever achieved stardom in so many sports as the remarkable Jim Thorpe. He *was* very special, as his mother and father and Pop Warner had believed him to be.

This greatness was officially recognized in 1950 —three years before his death—when James Francis Thorpe was voted the greatest athlete of the first half of the twentieth century. It was the proudest moment in the life of a great American athlete.